How To Find the **RIGHT MAN** *for* **YOU!**

by:

Jay Thomas

Illustrations by: Dan Maurice

Cover Design by: Susan Atkins

Published by: **J. D. THOMAS PUBLICATIONS**
P. O. Box 4208
Dayton, Ohio 45401

The opinions and recommendations given herein are based upon the author's experience and research believed to be accurate and reliable, but not infallible. The reader should necessarily act in her own best judgement.

Library of Congress Cataloging in Publication Data
Thomas, Jay, 1956-
How to Find the **RIGHT MAN** *for* **YOU!**
First Edition
1. Dating
2. Relationships
3. Self-improvement
4. Inspiration

ISBN 1-881312-00-3
Library of Congress Catalog Card Number: 92-093423

Table of Contents

I MET A SEASHELL TODAY

I met a seashell today,
He crawled right past the place I lay

It seemed a curious sight to me,
Him dragging his shell toward the sea

"Hello little fellow, why all the haste?"
But no reply, he quickened his pace

In a moment he disappeared into the salty blue,
leaving me all by myself. . . so what else is new?

Jay Thomas

DECIDE TO ACT!

Chapter 1

Getting Started

Today is going to be a wonderful turning point in your life! Although you may not be aware of it, before you stretches a golden path leading to unbelievable treasures. These treasures are new friends, new experiences, increased personal fulfillment, and ultimately, that very special someone you've been so patiently waiting to meet. With all this in your immediate future, no wonder today marks a significant turning point in your life!

In the following pages are the secrets to finding the man who's right for you. There is nothing complicated or mysterious about this process. Not only is the information in this book simple to follow, you will also discover how fun it is to break with your present routine. You will begin exploring the unlimited opportunities for enriching your social life far beyond what you ever imagined possible. You don't have to be rich, beautiful, or outgoing. Relax and be yourself. For the information in this book to work, you only need a sincere desire to find that special man. Your desire will be the spark that propels you through an exciting adventure into an astonishing world of discovery and promise.

No one can prevent you from taking this journey, but no one can make you take it either. This is something you must decide for yourself. If you decide not to act, then tomorrow, things will probably remain about the same as they are today. The same old routine and the same frustrating situations will continue to greet you each morning. On the other hand, you can choose to change your life and your future, molding them the way you want. After all, if you do not choose your future, others will do it for you. The future they give you will be to their liking, not necessarily to yours. Consequently, begin taking the positive actions revealed in this book. With a little determination, nothing will stop you from being successful. You have so much to gain!

It's Up to You

There is a false belief that somehow, someway, when you least expect it, that special man will one day magically appear. While it might be true that "Mr. Right" will come on the scene unexpectedly, you don't have to relinquish your fate to mere chance. There is nothing wrong with taking matters into your own hands. Many well meaning relatives and friends might advise you to be patient, saying, "When the time is right, he will come along." Let's be realistic, this may not happen. If it does, what guarantee do you have that this guy will be someone you want? This is an awful lot to leave to chance, isn't it?

Taking such a passive attitude is self-deceiving and actually increases the risk of settling for the wrong mate. Why not take an active role in this process and have the time of your life as well? It's not as difficult as you might think. This book will show you some very clever techniques and shortcuts for finding more potentially compatible men than you ever thought possible! Very shortly, you can be on your way to leading the kind of social life you always wanted. It's an adventure!

Here is your first step toward finding the man who's right for you: **develop an open mind and be eager to expand your horizons.** Be willing to try new things and meet new people. You have to have the pluck to take that first, scary step. Frequently, it's that first step that is the hardest. The second step will be much easier, the third more pleasant, and so forth until very shortly, you have all the excitement and challenge you want! Your current routine will become a thing of the past. In fact, your whole life will improve. One of the amazing bonuses of this adventure is that you will increase your capacity to enjoy what life has to offer and in turn, lead a happier, fuller life!

Your search for that special man will follow three simple guidelines: 1) Decide what kind of man you want and need; 2) look in all the right places; and 3) become active! It's as simple as that, easy and fun! You will discover how to do things the smart way and stop wasting precious time going in circles to nowhere. (Who knows, you may even decide you enjoy this process so much that you stay unattached and available!)

In the past, you may have convinced yourself that all the good men are already taken. Cheer up! This isn't true. In reality, there are just as many "good men" out there today as there were last year, and all the years past. What has actually happened is that you've become a little older and a little wiser; consequently, you've become more discerning. Your perception of which men are potentially compatible is better. You see things more objectively as you grow older. Consequently, you become more cautious about the kind of men you date. This is good! It is definitely a plus to be discerning when it comes to dating.

An Ounce of Prevention

Imagine you have decided to go shopping at a local mall. As you browse through the colorful, busy shops, various items begin to catch your eye — a new dress, a beautiful bedspread. Or perhaps it's jewelry you can't resist! Although it was originally your intention to just window shop, you now find yourself buying. As you drive home, doubts begin creeping into your mind, "Do I really need this? . . . Did I spend too much? . . . Should I take it back?"

Sure it's good to get out, enjoy some shopping and see what's out there. The problem is that stores and salespeople are all too skilled at helping you part with your money! Sometimes you wind up buying the merchandise they want you to have and not what you really want or need. No question about it, today's stores are effective environments for putting you in the spending mood through the subtle use of background music, attractive displays, easy payment plans, and SALES! Who can resist?

Fortunately, most stores will let you return unwanted merchandise and refund your money. You only suffer the inconvenience of a return trip to the mall and perhaps a wait in the customer service line. But when "shopping" for a potential mate, mistakes aren't so easy to correct. Years of hardship, emotional grief, and regret follow. Therefore, make certain, from the outset, you know exactly what qualities you are seeking in a man. It is imperative to learn how to recognize with which men you are truly compatible.* With a strong working knowledge of compatibility, successfully finding the right man for you will be easier.

Many women believe they know exactly what kind of man they want. But closer examination often reveals that these mental images of "Mr. Right" are not focused and too vague to help her in her search. The image of "Mr. Right" must be realistic and consistent with your true needs in a relationship. Here's an important point:

> **Once you've formed in your mind a clear, realistic image of the type of man you want, you will be well on your way towards finding him. Without this clear, realistic image, you severely limit your chances of finding and recognizing the man who's right for you!**

* Read: **Right Men, Wrong Men, Knowing the Difference.** Available through J. D. Thomas Publications.

DECIDE WHAT KIND OF MAN YOU WANT AND NEED

Chapter 2

Describe Your Ideal Man

Now it starts to get really interesting. Let's have some fun! In the following pages you will describe the kind of man you want to meet and date. You also get to dream a little about things you would like to do and things you want to accomplish in your life. Thinking about these issues is a vital part of finding "Mr. Right." So whatever you do. . . don't skip this section! You are going to put together some extremely important information about yourself. Without this information, it will be very difficult to point you in the right direction of potentially compatible men. The more objective and accurate your responses to the questions, the easier your search becomes.

Over the next few pages you will find a **Profile Questionnaire**. Set aside about 30 minutes to carefully answer the questions. Select a time and place where you will have quiet and privacy. The answers you give must be your sincere thoughts and reflect your honest feelings. Naturally, keep your answers private. There is no reason for you to reveal this personal information to others unless you choose to do so. Remember, these are your feelings and desires; no one else has a right to judge them.

When answering the questions, be sure not to leave any questions blank. If you do not immediately know an answer, think about the question or issue for a moment and then give your "best response." There are no questions intended to trick you. There are no right or wrong answers. This is simply your chance to pause and focus on where you want your life to go and the kind of man you would like to meet along the way. Have fun with the questions!

PROFILE QUESTIONNAIRE©

How To Find the **RIGHT MAN** *for* **YOU!**

Profile of "Mr. Right"

1. What do you find physically attractive in a man?

2. Describe the type of personality you are attracted to and feel most comfortable with.

3. Describe the type of career "Mr. Right" should lead.

4. What types of hobbies or recreation might he enjoy?

5. What educational background should he possess?

____

____

____

____

6. What should his core spiritual beliefs be?

____

____

____

____

7. What other qualities should he possess?

____

____

____

____

____

8. In order to meet and date compatible men, would you be willing to:

Visit new places?	❑ Yes	❑ No
Learn new things?	❑ Yes	❑ No
Meet new people?	❑ Yes	❑ No

Profile of Yourself
(A Snapshot of You Today)

1. What are your favorite things to talk about with friends?

____

____

____

____

2. What are your favorite activities?

____

____

____

____

3. Name your three most significant accomplishments in life.

____

____

____

4. Would you like to continue growing as a person and develop your abilities and talents?

❑ Yes ❑ No ❑ Undecided

Your Potential for Growth

(A glimpse of the future <u>you</u>!)

1. If you could change one thing about yourself, what would it be? Why?

   ____
   ____
   ____
   ____

2. If you could learn something new during the coming year, what would it be?

   ____
   ____

3. Name three things you want to accopmlish in the next 12 months?

   ____
   ____
   ____

4. How much effort and time are you willing to devote to accomplishing these goals?

   ❑ Very Little ❑ Some ❑ A Great Amount

Three Keys to Finding "Mr. Right"

If you took your time and carefully answered the **Profile Questionnaire**, you have complied some very valuable information about yourself. This information can help you to meet and date compatible gentlemen. The questionnaire is divided into three sections. The first section helps you define the type of man you want to find, the second section takes a quick snapshot of yourself, and the third section takes a look at opportunities for your personal growth. Each of these three sections asks probing questions. Your answers provide excellent clues which will assist you in your search.

Profile of "Mr. Right"

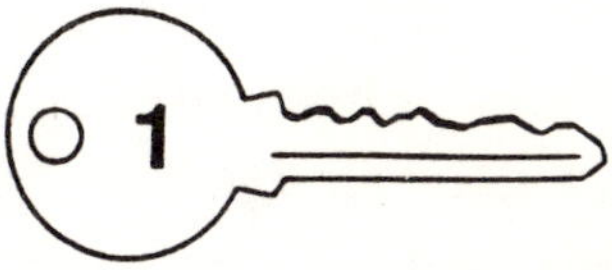

Clearly defining the type of man you want to meet and date is a wise thing to do. It is helpful to put into writing, the traits and qualities you seek. Doing this gives you greater control over your future. Finding compatible men to date is much easier once you clearly visualize the kind of man who is right for you.

Dating should involve your mind, as well as your heart. The heart does not think, it feels. This is why decisions on the basis of emotion alone are risky. By clearly defining the kind of man you want, you temper your emotions with good judgement. You become proactive and smart about the dating scene.

It should come as no surprise that finding compatible men will probably require some element of change in your life. You may have to visit new places, learn new things, and meet new people. Rather than feeling intimidated or nervous about these small risks, see them as exciting opportunities to experience life on a greater scale. Change is scary, but it can also be exciting. Without change, progress is impossible.

Profile of Yourself

Finding the right man for you begins with understanding yourself. You must recognize your interests and talents. It is difficult to realistically define the type of man you want and need until you first realistically see yourself. You are a wonderful, unique person. God only made one of you. Don't fight who you are. Accept your limitations and develop your gifts. If you aggressively pursue your natural talents, you will worry less about your weaknesses. It is amazing, but true:

> **When you follow your interests and talents in life, you will be more successful and contented. Moreover, you will magically attract compatible men to yourself. Discover what motivates and excites you, and your life will blossom in delightful and unexpected ways!**

Understanding this, you can quickly see why it is vital to join and participate in activities and organizations that energize you. Don't worry what others may think, find your niche and get involved!

Perhaps you aren't sure what your niche is or what particular activities are right for you. Often, a good way to discover your hidden talents is to list some of your past successes. No matter how small, every success has hidden within it common threads of personal talent. By listing these accomplishments together, you can frequently spot this talent. If not, show your list to some trusted friends and ask their opinion. It is exciting and wonderful to discover your gifts and talents. It is even more exciting to begin developing them.

In the questionnaire you were asked if you wanted to develop your abilities and talents and begin a program of personal growth. If your answer was "yes," then you are ready to begin your search for that special someone. Remember, progress requires change.

Your Potential for Growth

One of the most distinguishing features of living creatures is growth. While inanimate things decay and rust, living things grow and change. If you routinely feel bored or depressed, it might be an indication that your personal development is stagnating. Embarking on a program of personal development will combat those feelings of helplessness and frustration.

To lead a rewarding and challenging life, you must reach out and grasp opportunites. There are many ways to do this.

Perhaps you might enroll in classes or begin studying a subject that has long fascinated you. Or, you might begin a new hobby or sport. Your answers to the questionnaire indicate opportunities you ought to explore. It takes action and courage to begin a program of personal development, but the effort is worth the rewards. Before long, you can be enjoying a more fulfilling life and dating interesting, compatible men.

Three Keys to Finding "Mr. Right"

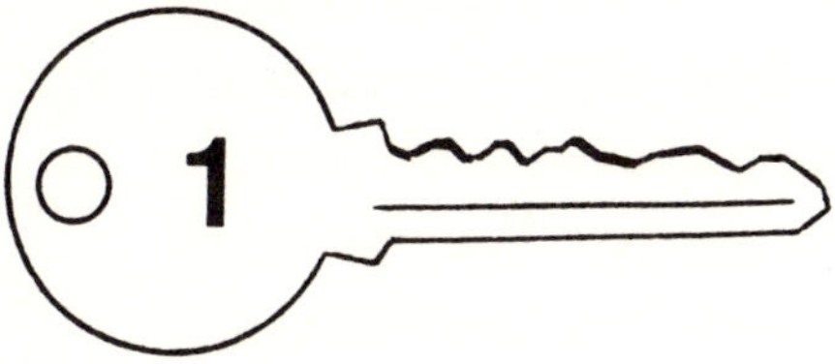

Clearly define the kind of man you want to find.

Understand yourself and recognize your interests and talents.

Look for opportunities for personal growth and development.

THE SECRET TO MEETING NEW MEN!

Chapter 3

New Horizons!

The following statement is very important. It represents your path to "Mr. Right":

> **Your ability to meet potentially compatible men is directly proportional to your rate of growth as a person and your willingness to embrace change.**

The more you explore new places and activities, the more people you will meet. It is impossible to grow without enlarging your circle of friends. You will find that as you grow, you begin meeting more and more people who are like yourself! You will be amazed at how similar your interests are, and how complementary your objectives seem to be. This isn't to say that every man you meet will be compatible with you. Life isn't this simple. However, you will begin to discover that you are meeting more and more men who appeal to you. There's no magic to all this; it is the basic nature of things. When you pursue activities that interest you, you meet others who share your interests. There is a natural tendency to find strong compatibility among people who share your interests.

The important issue is deciding which activities to pursue. This is a personal question and everyone's answer will vary. Fortunately, you have already provided your answer. The responses you gave in the Profile indicate some interesting areas for personal growth.

One of the most important factors in your growth will be your ability to meet and interact with people. The key to this is communication. The better you communicate, the better your interaction with other people. Conversation is the primary way you meet people, develop friendships, and build relationships.

The Art of Conversation

We all love to talk about things in life that interest us. The broader our range of interests, the more stimulating the conversation! Ever notice that people who bore us typically talk about the same things all the time? Their conversation is predictable. On the other hand, people who are popular and sought after are interesting people! We enjoy listening to them. They also tend to like listening to others. The art of conversation is a skill which, in many ways, directly effects our success. Our ability to win friends, find new jobs, gain promotions, and interact socially stems from our communication skills. The better we communicate the better we live!

Perhaps you are an excellent conversationalist and feel quite at ease talking with people, whether one-on-one or in front of large groups. If this is true, then you are at a significant advantage and should reap enormous benefits from this book.

However, you may be like many of us, uneasy speaking with new people and terrified of speaking in front of a large audience! The very thought of this may leave you cold. Ironically, this same fear masks a hidden world filled with tremendous advantages. Just think how far ahead in the game of life you'll be when you begin to feel comfortable expressing your desires and needs to others. Imagine how great it would be to walk into new situations and places and strike up lively conversations with people. Doing this with self-confidence and ease is a great boost to your personal growth. Without a measure of this ability, you will unnecessarily limit your success in both finding the man who's right for you and achieving your potential in life. This doesn't mean you have to become a great public speaker or be the "life of the party." Far from it! Instead, simply begin to develop your ability to converse.

This ability can begin with something as simple as a friendly, "Hello!" to a person whom you've passed many times in the hall but haven't had the courage to stop and make an introduction. From such humble beginnings come great things. If you want to develop your speaking skills and gain poise and self-confidence, consider promptly signing up for a speaking class. Now don't grumble or fidget. There's actually a good time awaiting you! There are many evening adult night schools and junior colleges offering these lessons at very affordable prices. In addition, you should seriously consider joining a local speaking club. As a rule, most speaking clubs maintain a friendly, encouraging atmosphere. These organizations have helped thousands of people improve their speaking abilities. You will have a lot of fun developing your speaking ability while making new friends at one of these classes or clubs. (It is interesting to note that these places are generally filled with more men than women . . . a little perk!)

With practice, you will discover that by enhancing your speaking ability, you attract and meet men with greater ease and frequency. Moreover, you will find that the quality of men you date will also change. Women who speak well and are self-assured in social settings are very appealing to most men. As mentioned before, this in no way implies that you have to assume some kind of charismatic personality or become the center of attention at social occasions. On the contrary, this is easily perceived for what it is — phoniness! Instead, you want to concentrate on refining your own natural personality and voice. If you are inherently quiet, then you can learn to express yourself in a reserved, yet self-assured manner. If you tend to be more outgoing, then this is all the more reason to ensure your conversation is polished!

Why not begin measures this very day to develop your conversational talents? Tonight, instead of filling your evening with television, call a friend or an old acquaintance and talk for a while. Talk about something you read in the paper or heard on the news that you think they might be interested in hearing. (Doing this will help you build self-confidence.) While you are near your telephone, pick up the phone book, call some of the local night schools, junior colleges, or speaking clubs and ask them to send you some literature on their classes and meetings. It only takes a moment to call and ask, but this little effort can pay off handsomely!

Learn Something New

Why not? In the **Profile Questionnaire**, you were asked, "If you could learn something new during the coming year, what would it be?" Perhaps you were able to write down some activity, hobby, class, or sport that you've always wanted to learn but have put off. As of now, the procrastination ends. Here's your chance to pursue one of your dreams!

Odds are, the answer you put down on the Profile, is something that catches your imagination and stimulates your sense of adventure. It might be taking an art class, learning a foreign language, or signing up for tennis lessons. Whatever it is, do it! The first step is always the hardest to take. It is easy to do nothing; taking action requires effort.

The possibilities for personal growth are endless and exhilarating! **Beginning today, develop a passion for adventure!** The biggest roadblocks impeding your desire to find and meet compatible men are routine and habit! Turn your television off and experience life for yourself. Don't limit this to only Fridays and Saturdays; you've got five other days in every week to tackle life for all it's worth! You can do it. What's more, once you start you'll wonder why you ever hesitated. Take the following week as an example:

Sunday	**AM**	Singles group at church
	PM	Evening dance and social
Monday	**PM**	French class
Tuesday	**PM**	Local book club meeting with guest author speaking
Wednesday	**PM**	Mixed bowling league
Thursday	**PM**	Your own personal time
Friday	**PM**	Your social club goes skating
Saturday	**PM**	Date with Jim (met him at Monday's French class!)

As you can see, the possibilities are vast. Only you choose your limits. (The woman in the example above seems to have endless energy and lots of free time to fill. You might not choose to move out so vigorously, and that's O.K. The important thing is to start experimenting. Break unproductive routines.)

How Routine & Habit Drain Your Life

Little Changes Can Invigorate Your Day!

on't stay up late atching TV. Go to ed early and awaken efreshed!

1. Wake up a little early, beat rush hour traffic.

. Join a pen pal club, write gentlemen you find interesting.

2. Seek new work projects where the old routine is broken and you can meet new, interesting people.

. On nights you stay in call new acquaintances, get to know people.

Result: Happiness, Fulfillment, Companionship

3. Take turns babysitting with a girlfriend. You'll get out more often and save money on babysitters.

4. Enjoy activities you like with friends.

Now, of course, you only have a limited amount of time and money, so pick and choose opportunities carefully. Wisely select those opportunities which hold the greatest promise and are most interesting. Choose activities which inspire and challenge you. Never get into the habit of going somewhere you dislike just to meet men. Doing this is a shortcut to nowhere and in the long run is quite frustrating. Be true to yourself and the results will be genuine.

Be realistic. Don't fall into the trap of trying to do so much that you wind up doing nothing well and everything halfway. Pace yourself. At first, add a couple of new activities to your life. Cultivate them for a while before adding another activity. Be willing to recognize (or admit) that an activity you've chosen isn't as fulfilling as you anticipated. Once this becomes clear, graciously bow out of the activity thus freeing yourself to pursue something else with greater potential. Be selective and be flexible!

Time is a limited resource. You don't have to always be in a hurry; but, don't throw your time away enduring meaningless activities. It is not selfish to quit an activity that drains your life without adding any benefit in return. It is frustrating to see the number of people trapped in terrible situations just because they've become so accustomed to them. It seems that **routine** and **habit** are the invisible masters of human destiny. People work at the same job because it is the only occupation they know. People live their entire lives in one town because that's where they've always lived. They eat the same foods day after day. And so the routine continues, day after day. Perhaps this is you.

Then one day, you get tired of it all. You ask yourself, "Is this all there is to my life?" Deep inside, you know you can do better. But those invisible masters, "routine" and "habit," whisper to you,

> "Better watch out! You don't know what you're getting into. It could be big trouble. Remember ten years ago when you tried ______________? Tisk, tisk. . . you should have known better. Did you ever mess things up then! Play it safe, don't rock the boat. Be happy with what little you have now. Don't risk it!"

Sound familiar? To see it in writing is almost comical, but the results of this kind of thinking are self-constraining. You want to act, yet something holds you back. Fear!

As a living being, you instinctively react to fear. Fear is a consuming force which can rob you of your dreams. Fear can assume many forms. There is fear of failure, fear of rejection, and fear of the unknown. If you give in to your fears, you will forfeit your dreams.

See fear for what it is, a normal reaction to uncertainty or perceived danger. The best strategy for dealing with fear is to identify exactly what it is about a situation that scares you. For example, if a stranger approaches you in a parking lot at night, you fear for your personal safety. Your instinctive reaction is to protect yourself.

On the other hand, you may be hesitant to join a new club or show up at a friend's party. In this instance, your protective instincts may be unfounded. A good way to conquer this type of fear is to tackle it in small pieces. Little triumphs build courage for bigger and better successes. That's why it is so important to take that first, small step. The first step might be calling for information about a club. Or, it might be signing up for a class you want to take. Whatever it is, be an explorer. Take those small, but significant opportunities to grow.

One Who Dared To Try

There once was a small, poor village nestled in a valley. The villagers were a proud but stubborn people. Towering over the village were majestic mountains, beautiful and awesome to behold. The village was hungry and times were bad. Stories were told of the bountiful fields and teaming streams on the other side of the mountain, yet no one would dare challenge the perilous cliffs to reach the other side. The mountains were high, the footing unsure, the risk too great. The villagers resigned themselves to endure another harsh winter rather than chance the unknown. All that is, but one.

There was one petite peasant girl who could not bear the thought of another cold, hungry winter. She explained to her neighbors the importance of exploring the hidden side of the mountain. To her dismay she received no encouragement, only rebuke. The other villagers had no interest in pursuing her dream of a better life, the risks were just too real for them to gamble their "secure" lives. She couldn't understand their reasoning. Winter was approaching and unless prompt action was taken, many would be lost to the coming barren season. It soon became apparent that the journey would be a lonely one. Undaunted, with determination and pluck, she set out.

The going was not easy. The rocks were cold and slick; she fell and bruised her knee: But she continued unshaken in her purpose. The higher she climbed, the wider the view. She could see so much more than she had ever seen before! Her village below became only faintly visible, one small hovel. Taking a deep breath, she continued her task. Slowly she inched her way up the treacherous slope. Finally, she reached the mountain's crest. Anxiously, she peered over the summit rocks into the valley below. Before her glistened a warm, inviting sun bathing a radiant forest. Meandering down the gentle slope into the lush woodland she was greeted by kind faces, others like herself who dared to face the unknown. In them she found a kindred spirit. This new land was more splendid than she could have ever dreamed. The doubts and fears she conquered were replaced with faith and courage. She would never be the same. She would never return to her old village.

Change is frightening, but it is necessary if we are to improve our lives. Complacency saps our vitality and traps us in our present circumstances. If you are not happy or satisfied with the way things are going in your life, then you must embrace change. **Change is your bridge to a better tomorrow!**

Why Change is Necessary

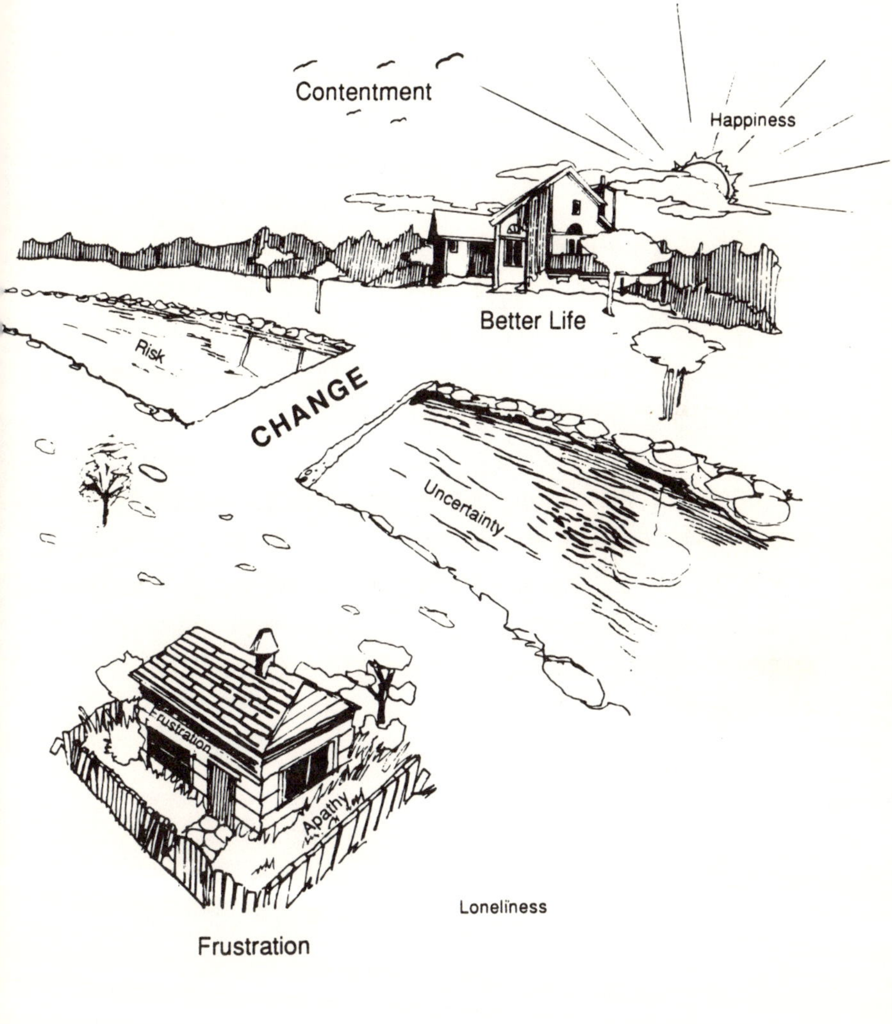

When life is frustrating, lonely, and boring, the only way to improve things is through change. Failure to make these changes keeps you in your current circumstances and holds you in your day-to-day rut. It is by making positive changes in your life that you grow as an individual and achieve a better life. Although change involves an element of risk and uncertainty, it is a small price to pay considering the wonderful riches awaiting you on the other side. Change is your bridge to a better tomorrow!

BECOME ACTIVE!

(Life shouldn't be a spectator event)

Chapter 4

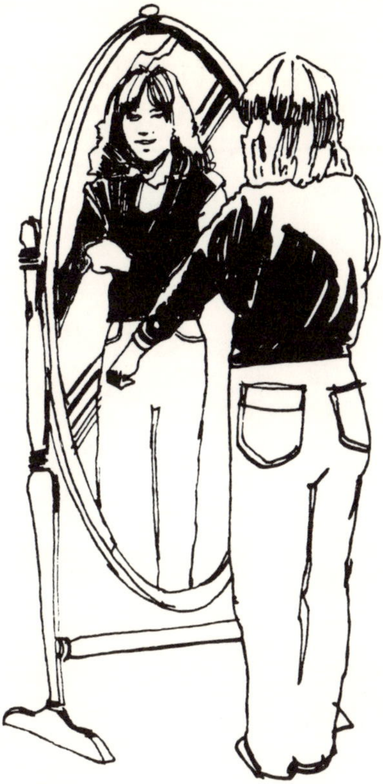

Opportunity Knocks!

The world is full of opportunity.* It's just waiting for you to take part. There's so much to do and see! In the pages to follow, lists are provided highlighting some of the many activities and opportunities available. There are five categories: Recreational and Social Activities, Sports and Athletics, Self-Improvement, Career Development, and Religious Activities. In some cases, a particular activity might be applicable to more than one category. In such instances, the activity is in the category most appropriately suited for helping you find compatible partners.

* Read: **25 Best Ways to Meet Terrific Bachelors!** Available through J. D. Thomas Publications.

Recreational and Social Activities

Walking	Camping
Hiking/Backpacking	Bicycling
Canoeing	Sailing
Ice Skating	Boating
Skiing	Windsurfing
Handgliding	Ballooning
Horseback Riding	Fishing
Archery	Bird watching
Trap and Skeet Shooting	Chess
Model Railroading	Photography
Gourmet Cooking	Pen Pal Writing
Community Service Organizations	Flying
Radio Controlled Airplanes and Cars	Bands
Travel and Tours	Dancing

Each of the pursuits listed under the Recreational and Social Activities category have spawned numerous clubs and organizations across the country and around the world. How do you find a local club? Let's take an example to explain.

Assume you are interested in joining a photography club. The first step is the telephone book; check the yellow pages under "Clubs" or "Social Organizations." No luck? Then look under the specific activity, in this case, "Photography."

If you still don't see any clubs or organizations listed, then call a local business in that field and ask for help. Often the business' proprietor will know firsthand where you can go to get involved. Using the example, calling one or two photographers will quickly put you right on track towards local photo clubs. But, let's assume you still haven't located a photo club.

If all else fails, find a current magazine related to photography and look for advertisements of clubs sponsoring your interests. Write down their addresses or phone numbers and contact them when you get home.

Actually, you'll probably find the information you're looking for easily. You can always locate these clubs with a little persistence, no matter how small the town you live in. You don't have to live in a big city to be socially active!

Sports and Athletics

Golf	Tennis
Volleyball	Swimming
Racquetball	Squash
Coed Softball	Coed Aerobics
Coaching Little League	Mixed Bowling
Mountaineering	Auto Racing
Surfing	Scuba
Martial Arts	Parachuting
Polo	Body Building
Coed Basketball	Running

The sports and athletic pursuits listed provide a broad range of involvement. At one end of the spectrum, you can enjoy a relaxing game of golf; at the other end, mountaineering or parachuting could be your thing! No assumptions about your personal athletic abilities or interests were made in composing the list. The primary objective is to give you a list of activities that tend to have large numbers of males involved. (After all, it's kind of tough finding compatible men in a ladies' aerobics class!)

You may not want to actively engage in some of the events, but you might be interested in watching. (For example, you may want to join an auto sports club and travel to some of the auto races held throughout the country.)

Another possibility is coaching, especially little leagues. You don't have to be a seasoned athlete to coach little league, you just have to like kids and have a measure of patience. Numerous women have discovered how much fun it is to coach little league T-Ball teams. The teams are usually composed of boys and girls between 4 and 6 years of age. They don't tend to be very skilled at the game; in fact, the real purpose of T-Ball is to teach the children sportsmanship and teamwork.

Each team generally has a head coach and several assistant coaches. T-Ball leagues constantly need adults to help supervise the kids and rarely turn down offers for assistant coaching. Once involved, you will have a great time watching the kids play, traveling to all their games, and meeting all the single fathers in your town!

Self-Improvement Activities and Classes

Archaeology	Astronomy
Basic Automotive	Video Making
Basic Computer	Ballroom Dancing
Drawing	Sculpting
Painting	Guitar
Entrepreneur Seminars	Woodworking
Free Lance Writing	Landscaping
Furniture Refinishing	Photography
Investment Seminars	Stock Market
French	Italian
Japanese	Spanish
German	Metalworking
Drama/Theater	Management
Speaking Improvement	Ham Radio

There's something for everybody here! Please notice that the self-improvement classes listed do not include sewing, weaving, pottery, weight loss, macramé, etc. There's nothing wrong with these activities, but you won't meet very many men. These classes tend to be female dominated.

On the other hand, with many of the classes or activities listed for self-improvement, you could very well find yourself the only woman participating. . . how's that for stacking the deck in your favor? Not only will you be meeting lots of new people, but you will be learning a useful skill and pursuing a long time interest of yours!

Another point worth mentioning is age. In some cases you might find yourself in a class or activity filled with men who happen to be younger than yourself. Don't write them off! You might be wise to consider the possibilities open to you with a younger male. Erase the old taboos from your mind. Men who date older women don't necessarily suffer from some obscure "mother's complex." If anything, it is an indication that the male is mature beyond his years and is capable of independent thought. These are positive qualities that reinforce a relationship.

Career Development

Accounting

Nursing

Biochemical Science

Telecommunications

Electrical Engineering

Education

Commercial Art

Journalism

Mechanical Engineering

Business Management

Social Work

Real Estate

Political Science

Aviation

Medicine

Behavioral Science

Chemistry

Computer Science

Counseling

Microbiology

Law

Marketing

Criminology

Music

Theater Arts

Labor Relations

Industrial Arts

Advertising

Again, the opportunities are endless. If you are inclined to pursue a new career (or expand your expertise in your current field), you should contact the appropriate educational institution. Write to the trade school, college, or university and request their curriculum catalog and admission procedures. If money is a problem, then tuition assistance is normally available. Write and investigate.

If you haven't already chosen a specific career path, then heed the following advice: follow careers that involve both your talents and your interests. Too many people pursue careers in fields they dislike just for the sake of money. Ironically, life tends to pull a twist of fate on these people. They eventually burnout or become frustrated.

Go with your instinctive desires. If you've always wanted to be a journalist, then be one! Have you secretly harbored a desire to be an actress? Do it! Don't let all the negatives in this world beat you before you even start! Sure, you may have to keep your present job while beginning your new career; that's only common sense. But, keep your ultimate goal in mind and pursue it with determination!

Religious Activities

Christian Fellowship Groups	Church Retreats
Singles Sunday School Classes	Gospel Concerts
Jewish Fellowship Groups	Bible Studies
Christian Universities	Support Groups
Religious Singles Groups	Church Outings

The opportunity to meet men who share your spiritual convictions may be a high priority for you. If so, locate some of the above groups and participate. Remember, however, that the primary purpose of these groups is religious in nature. While you can meet some wonderful men through them, this should not be your only reason for participating. But, if your spiritual life is important to you and you want a man who shares your faith, then this is an excellent way to increase your chances for meeting compatible men.

After looking over the lists of numerous activities and opportunities for personal growth and meeting new people, you probably noted several activities which caught your eye. Tonight, write down these activities and look up the phone numbers (or addresses) to contact for information regarding participation. Don't put it off! Call or write promptly. Don't be a victim of your own procrastination. Often, the hardest thing is taking that first, scary step. Once you've initiated action, it becomes much easier to follow through and become actively involved in improving your life and feeling more fulfilled. The potential rewards are enormous for those who decide to act.

These lists are by no means exhaustive. In fact, they only scratch the surface of possibilities. There is so much out there to explore! Your local newspaper probably has a special section listing clubs and organizations meeting each week. Make it a point to visit some of these meetings. If you look into one particular activity and find it's not what you want, then feel quite free to move on to another. That's what this book is all about, increasing your exposure to the world of possibilities and providing you with plenty of opportunity to form social networks. Social networks are extremely important tools for you to use in finding and screening potentially compatible partners. Let's take a closer look at this.

Social Networks

Social networks are very important. Basically, a social network is a collection of friends and acquaintances with whom you share common interests. For example, if you are interested in tennis, you can form a social network with others who are also interested in the sport. Forming a social network does not mean you have to establish some kind of club or hold periodic meetings. Rather, a social network is very informal; in fact, it can be no more than a collection of telephone numbers. Keeping your network simple is probably the best way to participate.

Forming a social network is quite easy. When you join a new activity, always ask to be included in any events the group might be planning. You can do this by making the request to the group's leader or to a friend you know in the group. Be sure to give your phone number (and if you feel comfortable in doing so, your mailing address for receiving activity notices). Remember, if you don't ask to be included, the group might forget to invite you. So don't automatically assume that everyone knows you want to actively participate. Never feel guilty or self-conscious about speaking up and voicing your desire to become involved with the group. You have every right to belong. If a particular organization is hesitant to include you, then seriously consider moving on to some other group or activity. Your purpose is to have fun, not endure rejection!

Once you become relaxed with your new group of friends and gain a measure of their trust, you can go one step further — help put together an outing. This will involve a little effort on your part, but the potential rewards are incredible! Let's say you have joined a German language class and have decided to help sponsor a social event. In keeping with the nature of your class, you could ask that everyone bring some type of German food. You might even have some polka tapes available to set the mood!

As the event's organizer, you will naturally want to telephone everyone to ensure they know the time, place, and what to bring. Since you will be calling everyone, you will have the opportunity to speak to all the men in your group. You will be surprised how easy it is to strike up a lively conversation with some of the guys you call. Best of all, since you are calling in reference to a group event, you don't have to worry about being considered too "forward" in contacting the gentlemen. Any welcome chit-chat that develops during your calls is an added benefit you can rightfully enjoy! You will be amazed at how many of the single guys will be delighted to hear from you. Don't be surprised if your phone calls initiate new friendships and interest. (Most men are very flattered when a woman calls to invite them to a party.)

Don't forget to call the ladies in your group, too. Failure to include your female friends will most likely ruin your party. As a matter of experience, the best parties tend to have a fairly even mix of men and women. By having a balance, more of your friends will enjoy the evening and be anxious to get together again.

Once you have formed your first social network and have experienced the process of becoming an active group member, you are ready to begin duplicating the network. This is done by joining another group and participating in it, too. For example, you might add an archaeology class to your schedule. As you become incorporated into this group, you might help sponsor a trip to a nearby excavation to dig for relics. Again, you'll be on the telephone making those important contacts.

The possibilities are phenomenal when you begin forming social networks! Never feel you have to put all your eggs into one basket. Branch out and explore several areas of interest at once. As you meet more and more people, your opportunities for meeting and dating compatible men will expand rapidly. Plus, you will discover some very interesting people along the way. Life will become anything but dull!

Eventually, if you are willing to tackle the challenge, you can begin forming the Mystery Network! This isn't for everybody, but if you are game for the unexpected, you might try it. To form a Mystery Network, you will host a group event. Request that everyone bring a friend or relative who has never experienced the particular activity you are hosting. When you do this, you can never predict how things will turn out. Usually, it is for the better. But be prepared for anything! One thing is for certain, the Mystery Network is a quick way to increase your number of acquaintances.

Perhaps thinking about the details of organizing social events and outings for groups leaves you a bit uneasy. Don't worry. It is not imperative that you take the lead in arranging these activities. You might feel more comfortable playing a

Social Networks are Wonderfu

Social networks are wonderful and powerful tools for enriching your dating life. There is no limit to the ways good social networking can help you expand your circle of acquaintances and friends. At first, your social networking efforts will make slow, gradual progress. However, before long, your efforts will compound and your social life will begin to take-off! You'll never be bored or lonely!

smaller role. If so, be an enthusiastic assistant! The important thing is to be active in the group and attend the functions regularly. In time, you will get to know the group and begin to relax around them. You may eventually feel more comfortable taking leadership roles in their outings. For now, the fact that you are getting out and exploring the world of opportunity is, in itself, a fantastic step!

Think of the incredible advantages associated with forming social networks. For each new network, you collect a new circle of friends and acquaintances. By slowly increasing the number of groups you participate in, you dramatically increase your opportunities for meeting compatible men. Moreover, if a particular group isn't holding your interest, you are always free to reduce (or terminate) your involvement with them. However, be careful to always replace your withdrawal from one group with entry into another, more interesting group. In this way, you maintain a maximum number of options. Doing this, your social life will prosper and you will find yourself growing as an individual.

Date Wisely

Before long you will be dating men who greatly appeal to you. At this point, you begin the most crucial step in finding the man who's right for you. You must learn to be objective in evaluating the men you date.

Dating is for fun! But, if your long term objective is to develop a lasting, healthy relationship, then you also need to keep your wits about you. Doing this requires two things. First, keep in your mind the clear, realistic mental image you defined in the **Profile Questionnaire**. Second, practice the self-assertiveness necessary to reject relationships not meeting your wants and needs.

Of course, this isn't to imply that you have to pick out every flaw in your dates and examine them under a microscope. Let's be realistic; men are human and, as such, imperfect creatures! Instead, take the time to objectively consider the men you date. See if they have the qualities you want. If you are seeking a man who has a good career, loves children, is romantic, and wants to live in the country, then step back and ask yourself if the man you are dating actually has these qualities. If the answer is an honest "yes," you are probably on the right track. Conversely, if you can't give an affirmative answer, it might be wise to reconsider the situation and be assertive.

You have to be true to yourself. In the long run, there is no gain in forming a relationship with someone incompatible with your desires in life. No one can make these decisions for you. You alone must decide whether or not someone is right for you. The best way to do this is sitting down and deciding beforehand which qualities and characteristics you do and do not want. Your **Profile Questionnaire** gave you the opportunity to do this. In order to stay true to your own needs, you are strongly urged to review your answers from the Profile once a day for the next two weeks. In this way you will establish a clear, realistic mental image of the man who's right for you.

Dating Safety

It is unfortunate that this book should have to include a section on Dating Safety. How nice it would be to live in a world where women are safe. It is an outrage that our country has become so violent and the price of life so cheap! However, we all know the realities that are out there.

You can go out, have the time of your life, and still do it safely. If you are going out to attend an activity in the evening, check out the neighborhood first. Ensure the area is well lighted and maintained. Call ahead of time to get an idea of the composition of the group you will be visiting. Whenever possible, take along a friend. You will be safer and probably feel less self-conscious entering a new group for the first time. When walking back to your car, always have your keys in hand. . . never wait until you get to your car to start searching through your handbag to find the keys. If you are nervous about going out to your car alone, ask one of the gentlemen (you trust) in the group to escort you to your car.

When dating, try to let someone else know where you are going, when you expect to return, and with whom you will be. If you live alone, call a friend or relative and let them know. Never let a man pressure you into situations or actions you do not want. You have every right to say "no" and have that request honored. If you find yourself in a situation that is rapidly going astray, remove yourself from that situation at once. No date is worth risking your personal safety. Should you ever discover someone following your car without your approval, do not drive home! Promptly drive to the nearest police station or fire house and report the incident. Wait until a patrolman arrives before driving off again. In this way, you prevent the individual from following you home or learning where you live.

Your safety is important. You can have a great time enjoying a rich social life if you temper your fun with a measure of caution. Remember, your trust is something a man must earn.

YOU ARE READY!

Chapter 5

How To Find the **RIGHT MAN** *for YOU!*

O.K., let's pull the ideas and suggestions in this book together into an overall Master Plan. With this plan, you will be ready to strike out on what can become your greatest adventure ever!

First, decide to act! This means you must decide in your own mind that you are willing to adjust your schedule, learn new things, go to new places, and meet new people. In other words, you must accept the need for positive change in your life. In order to come in contact with and meet compatible men, you have to break with your current routine and replace it with a more productive schedule and lifestyle. Remember, you cannot sit at home and expect "Mr. Right" to come to you. You must go out and become an active participant in life and, thereby, meet "Mr. Right" on his own turf. Once you decide to replace procrastination with action, things will start happening! The day you become determined to act is the day you begin to make positive improvements in your personal and social life. You must believe in yourself!

The second step is to **decide what type of man you want and need.** By carefully answering this question, you draw a road map to the man who's right for you. It's very difficult, if not impossible, to find the kind of man you want when you aren't sure exactly what his qualities and characteristics should be. For this reason, you must form in your mind a clear, realistic mental image of "Mr. Right." Once you have

How To Find the **RIGHT MAN** *for* **YOU!**

1. **Decide to act!**

2. **Decide what kind of man you want and need.**

3. **Become active (initiate a vigorous program of personal growth).**

4. **Accept change, fight routine!**

5. **Form social networks.**

6. **Date wisely and safely.**

7. **Enjoy!**

done this, it becomes easy to objectively evaluate men in light of their potential compatibility with you.

Next, **become active!** Embark on a program of personal growth. Begin seeking opportunities to explore new activities and hobbies that interest you. Do this by deciding to participate in recreational and social organizations, engaging in sports and athletics, taking self-improvement courses, or expanding your career potentials. By stepping out and putting yourself directly in the middle of the action, you significantly increase your chances for meeting potentially compatible men.

Learn to **accept change** as a natural element of life. Become comfortable with taking daily action to combat the routines and habits that unnecessarily constrain your world. Personal growth only comes when you venture beyond your "safe and secure" cocoon, spread your wings, and begin exploring the unknown.

Take advantage of the enormous rewards possible through the forming of **social networks.** Ask to be included in activities and outings. Arrange (or assist in arranging) special functions for your group. Use the telephone to call group members and invite them to functions you host. Become a friendly, industrious member of your group and enjoy the many social benefits that will inevitably come your way!

Date wisely. Enjoy your dates, but be realistic about long term compatibility issues. Never confuse infatuation with compatibility. You might meet a new and exciting man who greatly stimulates you. But take your time and sort through your emotions. Evaluate the qualities and traits in this individual. See if they align with your true needs and wants. Should this new male not fulfill your long term objectives and desires, then have the courage to admit this fact and treat the situation accordingly. On the other hand, if this man does match your clear, realistic image of "Mr. Right," then congratulations. . . you have discovered someone special!

A final word of encouragement is in order. Once you find the man who's right for you, continue your efforts toward personal growth and fulfillment. Don't drop anchor! After finding "Mr. Right" include him in your adventures and nurture a sense of teamwork and zest for life. As you sail into your new horizon, remember to keep your man as your shipmate and friend. Together, you will find the sailing much smoother!

THANK YOU!

I sincerely appreciate the opportunity to come into your life and present the information in this book. I trust it was helpful and uplifting. Life is so short; make it a point to live each day to the fullest. Follow your hopes and dreams, whatever they may be. My best wishes to you for a wonderful today and an even better tomorrow!

Jay Thomas

Please Return this Card, <u>your</u> opinions are important to us!

To receive information about our other exciting books, write to:

J. D. Thomas Publications
P.O. Box 4208
Dayton, OH 45401
or
Return this card and we will send you information.

Tear along dotted lines

CUSTOMER COMMENT CARD

***YOU* ARE AN *IMPORTANT* CUSTOMER!**

What you have to say is very important to us. Please take a moment to let us know how we are doing by filling out this form and dropping it in a mail box. We want to provide you with first-class service and the most helpful, interesting books possible.

BOOK: **How to Find the Right Man for You!**

	Very	Some	Not at All
Was this book helpful?	❑	❑	❑
Did you like this book?	❑	❑	❑

	Yes	No
Will you recommend this book to a friend?	❑	❑

Additional Comments/Suggestions:

____

____

____

____

Are there any book topics that you would like to see us publish?

____

____

____

❑ **Please send me *free* information about your other books!**

Name: ______________________________

Address: ______________________________

City/State/Zip: ______________________________

Your Date of Birth: ______________________________

Thank You!

Tear along dotted lines

VALUED CUSTOMER

NO POSTAGE
NECESSARY
IF MAILED
IN THE
UNITED STATES

BUSINESS REPLY MAIL

FIRST CLASS PERMIT NO. 44 DAYTON, OHIO

POSTAGE WILL BE PAID BY ADDRESSEE

Jay Thomas, Publisher
J. D. THOMAS PUBLICATIONS
P.O. Box 4208
Dayton, OH 45401-8837